BEST OF METALLICA

F HORN

Recorded by Scott Seelig

Cherry Lane Music Company
Director of Publications: Mark Phillips

ISBN: 978-1-60378-964-6

Visit our website at www.cherrylaneprint.com

CONTENTS

The Day That Never Comes

Music by Metallica
Lyrics by James Hetfield

F HORN

Enter Sandman

TRACK 2

Words and Music by
James Hetfield, Lars Ulrich and Kirk Hammett

F HORN

Fade to Black

Words and Music by
James Hetfield, Lars Ulrich,
Cliff Burton and Kirk Hammett

F HORN

Harvester of Sorrow

Words and Music by
James Hetfield and Lars Ulrich

F HORN

Nothing Else Matters

Words and Music by
James Hetfield and Lars Ulrich

HORN

One

TRACK 6

Words and Music by
James Hetfield and Lars Ulric

F HORN

Sad but True

Words and Music by
James Hetfield and Lars Ulrich

TRACK 7

F HORN

Moderately slow

Seek & Destroy

Words and Music by
James Hetfield and Lars Ulrich

F HORN **Moderate Rock**

The Thing That Should Not Be

Words and Music by
James Hetfield, Lars Ulrich and Kirk Hammett

HORN

Medium Rock

Repeat and fade

The Unforgiven

Words and Music by
James Hetfield, Lars Ulrich and Kirk Hammett

F HORN

Until It Sleeps

Words and Music by
James Hetfield and Lars Ulrich

F HORN

Welcome Home (Sanitarium)

Words and Music by
James Hetfield, Lars Ulrich and Kirk Hammett

F HORN

More Great Piano/Vocal Books

FROM CHERRY LANE

For a complete listing of Cherry Lane titles available,
including contents listings, please visit our web site at
www.cherrylane.com

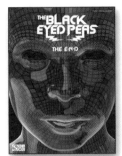

See your local music dealer or contact:

cherry lane
music company

EXCLUSIVELY DISTRIBUTED BY
HAL•LEONARD® CORPORATION
7777 W. BLUEMOUND RD. P.O. BOX 13819 MILWAUKEE, WI 53213

Prices, contents and availability subject to change without notice.

0512

METALLICA

Visit Cherry Lane Online at
www.cherrylane.com

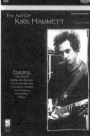

MATCHING FOLIOS

...AND JUSTICE FOR ALL
02506965	Play-It-Like-It-Is Guitar	$22.99
02506982	Play-It-Like-It-Is Bass	$19.95
02506856	Easy Guitar	$12.95
02503504	Drums	$18.95

DEATH MAGNETIC
02501267	Play-It-Like-It-Is Guitar	$24.95
02501312	Play-It-Like-It-Is Bass	$22.95
02501316	Easy Guitar	$15.95
02501315	Drums	$19.99

GARAGE INC.
02500070	Play-It-Like-It-Is Guitar	$24.95
02500075	Play-It-Like-It-Is Bass	$24.95
02500076	Easy Guitar	$14.95
02500077	Drums	$18.95

KILL 'EM ALL
02507018	Play-It-Like-It-Is Guitar	$19.99
02507039	Play-It-Like-It-Is Bass	$19.95

LIVE: BINGE AND PURGE
02501232	Play-It-Like-It-Is Guitar	$19.95

LOAD
02501275	Play-It-Like-It-Is-Guitar	$24.95

MASTER OF PUPPETS
02507920	Play-It-Like-It-Is Guitar	$19.95
02506961	Play-It-Like-It-Is Bass	$19.95
02506859	Easy Guitar	$12.95
02503502	Drums	$18.95

METALLICA
02501195	Play-It-Like-It-Is Guitar	$22.95
02505911	Play-It-Like-It-Is Bass	$19.99
02506869	Easy Guitar	$14.95
02503509	Drums	$18.95

RE-LOAD
02501297	Play-It-Like-It-Is Guitar	$24.95
02503517	Drums	$18.95

RIDE THE LIGHTNING
02507019	Play-It-Like-It-Is Guitar	$19.95
02507040	Play-It-Like-It-Is Bass	$17.95
02506861	Easy Guitar	$12.95
02503507	Drums	$17.95

ST. ANGER
02500638	Play-It-Like-It-Is Guitar	$24.95
02500639	Play-It-Like-It-Is Bass	$19.95

S&M HIGHLIGHTS
02500279	Play-It-Like-It-Is Guitar	$24.95
02500288	Play-It-Like-It-Is Bass	$19.95

PLAYERS

THE ART OF KIRK HAMMETT
02506325	Guitar Transcriptions	$17.95

THE ART OF JAMES HETFIELD
02500016	Guitar Transcriptions	$17.95

METALLICA'S LARS ULRICH
Book/CD Pack
02506306	Drum	$17.95

COLLECTIONS

BEST OF METALLICA
02500424	Transcribed Full Scores	$24.95

BEST OF METALLICA
02502204	P/V/G	$17.95

METALLICA: CLASSIC SONGS
Note-for-Note Transcriptions with DVD
Book/DVD Packs
02501626	Guitar	$19.99
02501627	Bass	$19.99
02501625	Drum	$19.99

5 OF THE BEST
02506210	Play-It-Like-It-Is Guitar – Vol. 1	$12.95
02506235	Play-It-Like-It-Is Guitar – Vol. 2	$12.95

LEGENDARY LICKS
An Inside Look at the Styles of Metallica
Book/CD Packs
02500181	Guitar 1983-1988	$22.95
02500182	Guitar 1988-1996	$22.95
02500180	Bass Legendary Licks	$19.95
02500172	Drum Legendary Licks	$19.95

LEGENDARY LICKS DVDS
A Step-by-Step Breakdown of
Metallica's Styles and Techniques
02500479	Guitar 1983-1988	$16.99
02500480	Guitar 1988-1997	$24.99
02500481	Bass 1983-1988	$16.99
02500484	Bass 1988-1997	$16.99
02500482	Drums 1983-1988	$16.99
02500485	Drums 1988-1997	$16.99

RIFF BY RIFF
02506313	Guitar Volume 1	$19.95
02500654	Guitar Volume 2	$19.95
02506328	Bass	$19.95

INSTRUCTION

METALLICA – EASY GUITAR WITH LESSONS
02506877	Volume 1	$14.95
02500419	Volume 2	$14.95

LEARN TO PLAY WITH METALLICA
Book/CD Packs
02500138	Guitar Volume 1	$15.95
02500885	Guitar Volume 2	$15.95
02500189	Bass Volume 1	$15.95
02500886	Bass Volume 2	$15.95
02500190	Drums	$14.95

UNDER THE MICROSCOPE
02500655	Guitar Instruction	$19.95

REFERENCE

METALLICA – THE COMPLETE LYRICS – SECOND EDITIONS
02501234	Lyrics	$9.99

Exclusively Distributed By

HAL•LEONARD®
CORPORATION
7777 W. BLUEMOUND RD. P.O. BOX 13819 MILWAUKEE, WI 53213

Prices, contents and availability
subject to change without notice.

cherry lane
music company

0712